DAILY KNITTING AGENDA

TO DO:

KNITTING PRIORITIES:

KNITTING QUOTE OF THE DAY:

KNITTING TAKS OF THE DAY

NOTES

DAILY KNITTING AGENDA

Date:

TO DO:

KNITTING PRIORITIES:

KNITTING QUOTE OF THE DAY:

KNITTING TAKS OF THE DAY

NOTES

DAILY KNITTING AGENDA

Date: _______________________

TO DO:

KNITTING PRIORITIES:

KNITTING QUOTE OF THE DAY:

KNITTING TAKS OF THE DAY

NOTES

DAILY KNITTING AGENDA

Date:

TO DO:

KNITTING PRIORITIES:

KNITTING QUOTE OF THE DAY:

KNITTING TAKS OF THE DAY

NOTES

DAILY KNITTING AGENDA

Date:

TO DO:

KNITTING PRIORITIES:

KNITTING QUOTE OF THE DAY:

KNITTING TAKS OF THE DAY

NOTES

DAILY KNITTING AGENDA

Date:

TO DO:

KNITTING PRIORITIES:

KNITTING QUOTE OF THE DAY:

KNITTING TAKS OF THE DAY

NOTES

DAILY KNITTING AGENDA

Date:

TO DO:

KNITTING PRIORITIES:

KNITTING QUOTE OF THE DAY:

KNITTING TAKS OF THE DAY

NOTES

DAILY KNITTING AGENDA

Date:

TO DO:

KNITTING PRIORITIES:

KNITTING QUOTE OF THE DAY:

KNITTING TAKS OF THE DAY

NOTES

DAILY KNITTING AGENDA

Date: _______________

TO DO:

KNITTING PRIORITIES:

KNITTING QUOTE OF THE DAY:

KNITTING TAKS OF THE DAY

NOTES

DAILY KNITTING AGENDA

Date:

TO DO:

KNITTING PRIORITIES:

KNITTING QUOTE OF THE DAY:

KNITTING TAKS OF THE DAY

NOTES

DAILY KNITTING AGENDA

Date: _______________

TO DO:

KNITTING PRIORITIES:

KNITTING QUOTE OF THE DAY:

KNITTING TAKS OF THE DAY

NOTES

DAILY KNITTING AGENDA

Date:

TO DO:

KNITTING PRIORITIES:

KNITTING QUOTE OF THE DAY:

KNITTING TAKS OF THE DAY

NOTES

DAILY KNITTING AGENDA

Date: _______________

TO DO:

KNITTING PRIORITIES:

KNITTING QUOTE OF THE DAY:

KNITTING TAKS OF THE DAY

NOTES

DAILY KNITTING AGENDA

Date:

TO DO:

KNITTING PRIORITIES:

KNITTING QUOTE OF THE DAY:

KNITTING TAKS OF THE DAY

NOTES

DAILY KNITTING AGENDA

Date:

TO DO:

KNITTING PRIORITIES:

KNITTING QUOTE OF THE DAY:

KNITTING TAKS OF THE DAY

NOTES

DAILY KNITTING AGENDA

Date:

TO DO:

KNITTING PRIORITIES:

KNITTING QUOTE OF THE DAY:

KNITTING TAKS OF THE DAY

NOTES

DAILY KNITTING AGENDA

Date:

TO DO:

KNITTING PRIORITIES:

KNITTING QUOTE OF THE DAY:

KNITTING TAKS OF THE DAY

NOTES

DAILY KNITTING AGENDA

Date:

TO DO:

KNITTING PRIORITIES:

KNITTING QUOTE OF THE DAY:

KNITTING TAKS OF THE DAY

NOTES

DAILY KNITTING AGENDA

Date: _______________

TO DO:

KNITTING PRIORITIES:

KNITTING QUOTE OF THE DAY:

KNITTING TAKS OF THE DAY

NOTES

DAILY KNITTING AGENDA

Date:

TO DO:

KNITTING PRIORITIES:

KNITTING QUOTE OF THE DAY:

KNITTING TAKS OF THE DAY

NOTES

DAILY KNITTING AGENDA

Date: _______________

TO DO:

KNITTING PRIORITIES:

KNITTING QUOTE OF THE DAY:

KNITTING TAKS OF THE DAY

NOTES

DAILY KNITTING AGENDA

Date: _______________________

TO DO:

KNITTING PRIORITIES:

KNITTING QUOTE OF THE DAY:

KNITTING TAKS OF THE DAY

NOTES

DAILY KNITTING AGENDA

Date: _______________

TO DO:

KNITTING PRIORITIES:

KNITTING QUOTE OF THE DAY:

KNITTING TAKS OF THE DAY

NOTES

DAILY KNITTING AGENDA

Date: _______________

TO DO:

KNITTING PRIORITIES:

KNITTING QUOTE OF THE DAY:

KNITTING TAKS OF THE DAY

NOTES

DAILY KNITTING AGENDA

Date:

TO DO:

KNITTING PRIORITIES:

KNITTING QUOTE OF THE DAY:

KNITTING TAKS OF THE DAY

NOTES

DAILY KNITTING AGENDA

Date:

TO DO:

KNITTING PRIORITIES:

KNITTING QUOTE OF THE DAY:

KNITTING TAKS OF THE DAY

NOTES

DAILY KNITTING AGENDA

Date: ________________

TO DO:

KNITTING PRIORITIES:

KNITTING QUOTE OF THE DAY:

KNITTING TAKS OF THE DAY

NOTES

DAILY KNITTING AGENDA

Date:

TO DO:

KNITTING PRIORITIES:

KNITTING QUOTE OF THE DAY:

KNITTING TAKS OF THE DAY

NOTES

DAILY KNITTING AGENDA

Date: _______________

TO DO:

KNITTING PRIORITIES:

KNITTING QUOTE OF THE DAY:

KNITTING TAKS OF THE DAY

NOTES

DAILY KNITTING AGENDA

Date:

TO DO:

KNITTING PRIORITIES:

KNITTING QUOTE OF THE DAY:

KNITTING TAKS OF THE DAY

NOTES

DAILY KNITTING AGENDA

Date: _______________________

TO DO:

KNITTING PRIORITIES:

KNITTING QUOTE OF THE DAY:

KNITTING TAKS OF THE DAY

NOTES

DAILY KNITTING AGENDA

Date:

TO DO:

KNITTING PRIORITIES:

KNITTING QUOTE OF THE DAY:

KNITTING TAKS OF THE DAY

NOTES

DAILY KNITTING AGENDA

Date:

TO DO:

KNITTING PRIORITIES:

KNITTING QUOTE OF THE DAY:

KNITTING TAKS OF THE DAY

NOTES

DAILY KNITTING AGENDA

Date:

TO DO:

KNITTING PRIORITIES:

KNITTING QUOTE OF THE DAY:

KNITTING TAKS OF THE DAY

NOTES

DAILY KNITTING AGENDA

Date:

TO DO:

KNITTING PRIORITIES:

KNITTING QUOTE OF THE DAY:

KNITTING TAKS OF THE DAY

NOTES

DAILY KNITTING AGENDA

Date:

TO DO:

KNITTING PRIORITIES:

KNITTING QUOTE OF THE DAY:

KNITTING TAKS OF THE DAY

NOTES

DAILY KNITTING AGENDA

Date:

TO DO:

KNITTING PRIORITIES:

KNITTING QUOTE OF THE DAY:

KNITTING TAKS OF THE DAY

NOTES

DAILY KNITTING AGENDA

Date:

TO DO:

KNITTING PRIORITIES:

KNITTING QUOTE OF THE DAY:

KNITTING TAKS OF THE DAY

NOTES

DAILY KNITTING AGENDA

Date: _______________

TO DO:

KNITTING PRIORITIES:

KNITTING QUOTE OF THE DAY:

KNITTING TAKS OF THE DAY

NOTES

DAILY KNITTING AGENDA

Date:

TO DO:

KNITTING PRIORITIES:

KNITTING QUOTE OF THE DAY:

KNITTING TAKS OF THE DAY

NOTES

DAILY KNITTING AGENDA

Date:

TO DO:

KNITTING PRIORITIES:

KNITTING QUOTE OF THE DAY:

KNITTING TAKS OF THE DAY

NOTES

DAILY KNITTING AGENDA

Date:

TO DO:

KNITTING PRIORITIES:

KNITTING QUOTE OF THE DAY:

KNITTING TAKS OF THE DAY

NOTES

DAILY KNITTING AGENDA

Date: _______________

TO DO:

KNITTING PRIORITIES:

KNITTING QUOTE OF THE DAY:

KNITTING TAKS OF THE DAY

NOTES

DAILY KNITTING AGENDA

Date:

TO DO:

KNITTING PRIORITIES:

KNITTING QUOTE OF THE DAY:

KNITTING TAKS OF THE DAY

NOTES

DAILY KNITTING AGENDA

Date:

TO DO:

KNITTING PRIORITIES:

KNITTING QUOTE OF THE DAY:

KNITTING TAKS OF THE DAY

NOTES

DAILY KNITTING AGENDA

Date:

TO DO:

KNITTING PRIORITIES:

KNITTING QUOTE OF THE DAY:

KNITTING TAKS OF THE DAY

NOTES

DAILY KNITTING AGENDA

Date: _______________

TO DO:

KNITTING PRIORITIES:

KNITTING QUOTE OF THE DAY:

KNITTING TAKS OF THE DAY

NOTES

DAILY KNITTING AGENDA

Date:

TO DO:

KNITTING PRIORITIES:

KNITTING QUOTE OF THE DAY:

KNITTING TAKS OF THE DAY

NOTES

DAILY KNITTING AGENDA

Date:

TO DO:

KNITTING PRIORITIES:

KNITTING QUOTE OF THE DAY:

KNITTING TAKS OF THE DAY

NOTES

DAILY KNITTING AGENDA

Date:

TO DO:

KNITTING PRIORITIES:

KNITTING QUOTE OF THE DAY:

KNITTING TAKS OF THE DAY

NOTES

DAILY KNITTING AGENDA

Date:

TO DO:

KNITTING PRIORITIES:

KNITTING QUOTE OF THE DAY:

KNITTING TAKS OF THE DAY

NOTES

DAILY KNITTING AGENDA

Date:

TO DO:

KNITTING PRIORITIES:

KNITTING QUOTE OF THE DAY:

KNITTING TAKS OF THE DAY

NOTES

DAILY KNITTING AGENDA

Date:

TO DO:

KNITTING PRIORITIES:

KNITTING QUOTE OF THE DAY:

KNITTING TAKS OF THE DAY

NOTES

DAILY KNITTING AGENDA

Date:

TO DO:

KNITTING PRIORITIES:

KNITTING QUOTE OF THE DAY:

KNITTING TAKS OF THE DAY

NOTES

DAILY KNITTING AGENDA

Date: _______________________

TO DO:

KNITTING PRIORITIES:

KNITTING QUOTE OF THE DAY:

KNITTING TAKS OF THE DAY

NOTES

DAILY KNITTING AGENDA

Date:

TO DO:

KNITTING PRIORITIES:

KNITTING QUOTE OF THE DAY:

KNITTING TAKS OF THE DAY

NOTES

DAILY KNITTING AGENDA

Date:

TO DO:

KNITTING PRIORITIES:

KNITTING QUOTE OF THE DAY:

KNITTING TAKS OF THE DAY

NOTES

DAILY KNITTING AGENDA

Date:

TO DO:

KNITTING PRIORITIES:

KNITTING QUOTE OF THE DAY:

KNITTING TAKS OF THE DAY

NOTES

DAILY KNITTING AGENDA

Date:

TO DO:

KNITTING PRIORITIES:

KNITTING QUOTE OF THE DAY:

KNITTING TAKS OF THE DAY

NOTES

DAILY KNITTING AGENDA

Date:

TO DO:

KNITTING PRIORITIES:

KNITTING QUOTE OF THE DAY:

KNITTING TAKS OF THE DAY

NOTES

DAILY KNITTING AGENDA

Date:

TO DO:

KNITTING PRIORITIES:

KNITTING QUOTE OF THE DAY:

KNITTING TAKS OF THE DAY

NOTES

DAILY KNITTING AGENDA

Date:

TO DO:

KNITTING PRIORITIES:

KNITTING QUOTE OF THE DAY:

KNITTING TAKS OF THE DAY

NOTES

DAILY KNITTING AGENDA

Date: _______________________

TO DO:

KNITTING PRIORITIES:

KNITTING QUOTE OF THE DAY:

KNITTING TAKS OF THE DAY

NOTES

DAILY KNITTING AGENDA

Date:

TO DO:

KNITTING PRIORITIES:

KNITTING QUOTE OF THE DAY:

KNITTING TAKS OF THE DAY

NOTES

DAILY KNITTING AGENDA

Date: _______________

TO DO:

KNITTING PRIORITIES:

KNITTING QUOTE OF THE DAY:

KNITTING TAKS OF THE DAY

NOTES

DAILY KNITTING AGENDA

Date:

TO DO:

KNITTING PRIORITIES:

KNITTING QUOTE OF THE DAY:

KNITTING TAKS OF THE DAY

NOTES

DAILY KNITTING AGENDA

Date: _______________

TO DO:

KNITTING PRIORITIES:

KNITTING QUOTE OF THE DAY:

KNITTING TAKS OF THE DAY

NOTES

DAILY KNITTING AGENDA

Date:

TO DO:

KNITTING PRIORITIES:

KNITTING QUOTE OF THE DAY:

KNITTING TAKS OF THE DAY

NOTES

DAILY KNITTING AGENDA

Date: _______________

TO DO:

KNITTING PRIORITIES:

KNITTING QUOTE OF THE DAY:

KNITTING TAKS OF THE DAY

NOTES

DAILY KNITTING AGENDA

Date:

TO DO:

KNITTING PRIORITIES:

KNITTING QUOTE OF THE DAY:

KNITTING TAKS OF THE DAY

NOTES

DAILY KNITTING AGENDA

Date:

TO DO:

KNITTING PRIORITIES:

KNITTING QUOTE OF THE DAY:

KNITTING TAKS OF THE DAY

NOTES

DAILY KNITTING AGENDA

Date: _______________

TO DO:

KNITTING PRIORITIES:

KNITTING QUOTE OF THE DAY:

KNITTING TAKS OF THE DAY

NOTES

DAILY KNITTING AGENDA

Date: _______________

TO DO:

KNITTING PRIORITIES:

KNITTING QUOTE OF THE DAY:

KNITTING TAKS OF THE DAY

NOTES

DAILY KNITTING AGENDA

Date:

TO DO:

KNITTING PRIORITIES:

KNITTING QUOTE OF THE DAY:

KNITTING TAKS OF THE DAY

NOTES

DAILY KNITTING AGENDA

Date:

TO DO:

KNITTING PRIORITIES:

KNITTING QUOTE OF THE DAY:

KNITTING TAKS OF THE DAY

NOTES

DAILY KNITTING AGENDA

Date:

TO DO:

KNITTING PRIORITIES:

KNITTING QUOTE OF THE DAY:

KNITTING TAKS OF THE DAY

NOTES

DAILY KNITTING AGENDA

Date: _______________

TO DO:

KNITTING PRIORITIES:

KNITTING QUOTE OF THE DAY:

KNITTING TAKS OF THE DAY

NOTES

DAILY KNITTING AGENDA

Date:

TO DO:

KNITTING PRIORITIES:

KNITTING QUOTE OF THE DAY:

KNITTING TAKS OF THE DAY

NOTES

DAILY KNITTING AGENDA

Date: _______________________

TO DO:

KNITTING PRIORITIES:

KNITTING QUOTE OF THE DAY:

KNITTING TAKS OF THE DAY

NOTES

DAILY KNITTING AGENDA

Date:

TO DO:

KNITTING PRIORITIES:

KNITTING QUOTE OF THE DAY:

KNITTING TAKS OF THE DAY

NOTES

DAILY KNITTING AGENDA

Date:

TO DO:

KNITTING PRIORITIES:

KNITTING QUOTE OF THE DAY:

KNITTING TAKS OF THE DAY

NOTES

DAILY KNITTING AGENDA

Date: _______________

TO DO:

KNITTING PRIORITIES:

KNITTING QUOTE OF THE DAY:

KNITTING TAKS OF THE DAY

NOTES

DAILY KNITTING AGENDA

Date: ___________________

TO DO:

KNITTING PRIORITIES:

KNITTING QUOTE OF THE DAY:

KNITTING TAKS OF THE DAY

NOTES

DAILY KNITTING AGENDA

Date:

TO DO:

KNITTING PRIORITIES:

KNITTING QUOTE OF THE DAY:

KNITTING TAKS OF THE DAY

NOTES

DAILY KNITTING AGENDA

Date: _______________

TO DO:

KNITTING PRIORITIES:

KNITTING QUOTE OF THE DAY:

KNITTING TAKS OF THE DAY

NOTES

DAILY KNITTING AGENDA

Date:

TO DO:

KNITTING PRIORITIES:

KNITTING QUOTE OF THE DAY:

KNITTING TAKS OF THE DAY

NOTES

DAILY KNITTING AGENDA

Date:

TO DO:

KNITTING PRIORITIES:

KNITTING QUOTE OF THE DAY:

KNITTING TAKS OF THE DAY

NOTES

DAILY KNITTING AGENDA

Date:

TO DO:

KNITTING PRIORITIES:

KNITTING QUOTE OF THE DAY:

KNITTING TAKS OF THE DAY

NOTES

DAILY KNITTING AGENDA

Date: ______________________

TO DO:

KNITTING PRIORITIES:

KNITTING QUOTE OF THE DAY:

KNITTING TAKS OF THE DAY

NOTES

DAILY KNITTING AGENDA

Date: _______________

TO DO:

KNITTING PRIORITIES:

KNITTING QUOTE OF THE DAY:

KNITTING TAKS OF THE DAY

NOTES

DAILY KNITTING AGENDA

Date: _______________

TO DO:

KNITTING PRIORITIES:

KNITTING QUOTE OF THE DAY:

KNITTING TAKS OF THE DAY

NOTES

DAILY KNITTING AGENDA

Date:

TO DO:

KNITTING PRIORITIES:

KNITTING QUOTE OF THE DAY:

KNITTING TAKS OF THE DAY

NOTES

DAILY KNITTING AGENDA

Date:

TO DO:

KNITTING PRIORITIES:

KNITTING QUOTE OF THE DAY:

KNITTING TAKS OF THE DAY

NOTES

DAILY KNITTING AGENDA

Date:

TO DO:

KNITTING PRIORITIES:

KNITTING QUOTE OF THE DAY:

KNITTING TAKS OF THE DAY

NOTES

DAILY KNITTING AGENDA

Date: _______________

TO DO:

KNITTING PRIORITIES:

KNITTING QUOTE OF THE DAY:

KNITTING TAKS OF THE DAY

NOTES

DAILY KNITTING AGENDA

Date:

TO DO:

KNITTING PRIORITIES:

KNITTING QUOTE OF THE DAY:

KNITTING TAKS OF THE DAY

NOTES

DAILY KNITTING AGENDA

Date: ______________________

TO DO:

KNITTING PRIORITIES:

KNITTING QUOTE OF THE DAY:

KNITTING TAKS OF THE DAY

NOTES

DAILY KNITTING AGENDA

Date:

TO DO:

KNITTING PRIORITIES:

KNITTING QUOTE OF THE DAY:

KNITTING TAKS OF THE DAY

NOTES

DAILY KNITTING AGENDA

Date: _______________

TO DO:

KNITTING PRIORITIES:

KNITTING QUOTE OF THE DAY:

KNITTING TAKS OF THE DAY

NOTES

DAILY KNITTING AGENDA

Date:

TO DO:

KNITTING PRIORITIES:

KNITTING QUOTE OF THE DAY:

KNITTING TAKS OF THE DAY

NOTES

DAILY KNITTING AGENDA

Date: _______________

TO DO: ~

KNITTING PRIORITIES:

KNITTING QUOTE OF THE DAY:

KNITTING TAKS OF THE DAY

NOTES

DAILY KNITTING AGENDA

Date:

TO DO:

KNITTING PRIORITIES:

KNITTING QUOTE OF THE DAY:

KNITTING TAKS OF THE DAY

NOTES

DAILY KNITTING AGENDA

Date:

TO DO:

KNITTING PRIORITIES:

KNITTING QUOTE OF THE DAY:

KNITTING TAKS OF THE DAY

NOTES

DAILY KNITTING AGENDA

Date:

TO DO:

KNITTING PRIORITIES:

KNITTING QUOTE OF THE DAY:

KNITTING TAKS OF THE DAY

NOTES

DAILY KNITTING AGENDA

Date:

TO DO:

KNITTING PRIORITIES:

KNITTING QUOTE OF THE DAY:

KNITTING TAKS OF THE DAY

NOTES

DAILY KNITTING AGENDA

Date:

TO DO:

KNITTING PRIORITIES:

KNITTING QUOTE OF THE DAY:

KNITTING TAKS OF THE DAY

NOTES

DAILY KNITTING AGENDA

Date:

TO DO:

KNITTING PRIORITIES:

KNITTING QUOTE OF THE DAY:

KNITTING TAKS OF THE DAY

NOTES

DAILY KNITTING AGENDA

Date:

TO DO:

KNITTING PRIORITIES:

KNITTING QUOTE OF THE DAY:

KNITTING TAKS OF THE DAY

NOTES

DAILY KNITTING AGENDA

Date: _______________

TO DO:

KNITTING PRIORITIES:

KNITTING QUOTE OF THE DAY:

KNITTING TAKS OF THE DAY

NOTES

DAILY KNITTING AGENDA

Date: _______________

TO DO:

KNITTING PRIORITIES:

KNITTING QUOTE OF THE DAY:

KNITTING TAKS OF THE DAY

NOTES

DAILY KNITTING AGENDA

Date:

TO DO:

KNITTING PRIORITIES:

KNITTING QUOTE OF THE DAY:

KNITTING TAKS OF THE DAY

NOTES

DAILY KNITTING AGENDA

Date:

TO DO:

KNITTING PRIORITIES:

KNITTING QUOTE OF THE DAY:

KNITTING TAKS OF THE DAY

NOTES

DAILY KNITTING AGENDA

Date: _______________

TO DO:

KNITTING PRIORITIES:

KNITTING QUOTE OF THE DAY:

KNITTING TAKS OF THE DAY

NOTES

DAILY KNITTING AGENDA

Date:

TO DO:

KNITTING PRIORITIES:

KNITTING QUOTE OF THE DAY:

KNITTING TAKS OF THE DAY

NOTES

DAILY KNITTING AGENDA

Date: _______________

TO DO:

KNITTING PRIORITIES:

KNITTING QUOTE OF THE DAY:

KNITTING TAKS OF THE DAY

NOTES

DAILY KNITTING AGENDA

Date:

TO DO:

KNITTING PRIORITIES:

KNITTING QUOTE OF THE DAY:

KNITTING TAKS OF THE DAY

NOTES

DAILY KNITTING AGENDA

Date:

TO DO:

KNITTING PRIORITIES:

KNITTING QUOTE OF THE DAY:

KNITTING TAKS OF THE DAY

NOTES

DAILY KNITTING AGENDA

Date:

TO DO:

KNITTING PRIORITIES:

KNITTING QUOTE OF THE DAY:

KNITTING TAKS OF THE DAY

NOTES

DAILY KNITTING AGENDA

Date: _______________

TO DO:

KNITTING PRIORITIES:

KNITTING QUOTE OF THE DAY:

KNITTING TAKS OF THE DAY

NOTES

DAILY KNITTING AGENDA

Date:

TO DO:

KNITTING PRIORITIES:

KNITTING QUOTE OF THE DAY:

KNITTING TAKS OF THE DAY

NOTES